ARGUMENT

IN BEHALF OF

Hon. ALBERT D. BRIGGS,

RAILROAD COMMISSIONER,

BEFORE THE

COMMITTEE ON RAILROADS OF THE MASSACHUSETTS LEGISLATURE.

March 28, 1876.

By CHARLES ALLEN.

BOSTON:
WRIGHT & POTTER, STATE PRINTERS,
79 Milk Street (corner of Federal).
1876.

ARGUMENT.

Mr. Chairman and Gentlemen of the Committee:

This investigation has its origin partly, I suppose, in the desire of certain persons, who have felt the fidelity of Mr. Briggs as a public officer, to get rid of him, because they are not able to meet his official requirements of them, and of their railroads; and partly, no doubt, in the honest desire of the people of Massachusetts that their public servants shall be above suspicion. I need not concern myself, in discussing the testimony which has been laid before the Committee, with the first class of people, because I sympathize most fully with every desire which the most jealous person entertains that the civil service of Massachusetts shall be above reproach, and especially at this time, when there seems to be corruption in the air at Washington. It is of importance to the safety of the Commonwealth that corruption, if it exists in Massachusetts, should be exposed. But, Mr. Chairman and gentlemen, if corruption does not exist, then it is almost of equal importance that the integrity and the honesty of faithful public servants in Massachusetts shall not be brought into reproach; because the chief of the treasures of Massachusetts is not in its accumulated wealth, nor yet in its noble institutions of religion, charity and learning, but it is in the character of its citizens. While it is well that the spirit of inquiry, of suspicion even, should be abroad, yet where there is nothing but honesty and fidelity, then this spirit of inquiry and suspicion should prove a shield to protect the innocent, as well as a sword to slay the guilty. It is a matter of general concern that the reputation of citizens of Massachusetts who hold public office shall not suffer unjustly, and now, of all times, I have no doubt you will appreciate and feel that if nothing has appeared in the course of this case which exposes Mr. Briggs to any censure, then it will be a pleasure to allow him to enjoy hereafter, as he has in the past, the full confidence and esteem of the public. You will not care to send forth word to the world that a public officer of Massachusetts is brought into discredit, and that the fair fame of the State is tarnished.

In the first place, I am happy to say, there has not been shown before you, any actual want of integrity, any official corruption, on the part of Mr. Briggs. There is not even a charge or suggestion of the sort. Nor is it said to you, nor intimated by any person, that there has been shown in his official conduct any bias in favor of any railroad corporation over which he has official supervision, or any prejudice against any corporation. No railroad corporation is here complaining, and no person is here complaining that the public interests have suffered at all in either of these respects,—that he has been either too lenient or too severe in the discharge of his duty. In addition, there is nothing here to show that there has been, in the discharge of his official duty, any neglect or incompetence. No broken-down bridges attest, during his term of office, any lack of fidelity on the part of the board of which he is a member. There has been no loss of human life in Massachusetts, during the four years of his term of office, which comes up here to cry out against him. No, gentlemen, he has discharged his duty with fidelity and efficiency in that respect. There has been no railroad accident, no broken-down bridge in Massachusetts, that has been directly or indirectly traceable to any neglect of his. There is nothing of the sort; and I think I may say that whatever is, or can be alleged against Mr. Briggs, will be found to rest ultimately on this: that he has put upon the law a wrong construction. Whether he has done so or not, I will discuss hereafter. But for the general integrity, honesty, fidelity, efficiency of his official management, there is not only nothing here inculpating him to any extent, on the part of any witness, but you have the positive evidence of his associates and of other witnesses, of Mr. Bill, Mr. Washburn, Mr. Stoddard, Mr. Harris, and others; and there might have been, if we had asked them to come, a cloud of witnesses, to testify, so far as their knowledge extends, so far as their opinions reached, that his course was wholly above reproach.

So, also, I feel entirely strong in saying that in addition to this general and noble vindication of his character, there is nothing here to show that he has ever used his official position in any way to secure private business for himself or for his firm. If his construction of the law was correct, that it is permissible for his firm to enter into competition for the building of railroad bridges for railroad corporations in Massachusetts, then, of course, it follows that the mere fact of his firm's obtaining some business raises no presumption against him. Some business would naturally go to his firm. You will not fail to observe that this is not a case where they have inaugurated any new business. It is the case of an old, established firm. They have been in business many years; they have been in partnership together for a considerable number of years; and, of course, if he is under the law allowed to continue his business, to engage in competition with other firms for railroad work, then no presumption rests against him from the fact that some work comes to him; of course some work will come to him, and some work will go to others. What I mean to say is this: there is nothing in this case to show that he has ever used his official influence to divert business to his firm, and, on the other hand, it appears by the direct testimony of various witnesses that he has abstained from so doing; from the testimony of Mr. Bill, from the testimony of Mr. Stoddard, of Mr. Folsom, of the Boston & Providence Railroad Company, of Mr. Munson, of Gov. Stearns, and, perhaps, one or two others, to that effect. Besides that, there are certain facts in this case which will enable me to go considerably further than content myself with a mere negative statement that he has not used his official position wrongly. There is the testimony of Mr. Bill and of Mr. Hawkins, that on a $9,000 contract in competition with A. D. Briggs & Co., Mr. Hawkins got the contract by underbidding only $15. There is also the testimony of Mr. Briggs, that out of one hundred and fifty bridges in Massachusetts, of railroad corporations, where the board of commissioners have felt it their duty to express their opinion that they were unsafe, or ought to be made stronger to insure their safety, his firm have not rebuilt a single one, while Mr. Hawkins and their other competitors have rebuilt some, and the railroad companies others. There is, in addition to this, testimony that during the four years he has held office—four years and over, now—of all the bridges that have been built in Massachusetts during that time for railroad companies, the only railroad bridge built by his firm has been that on the Boston & Providence Railroad at Hyde Park. So that I think these facts justify me in saying to you, that not only he has used no official influence to direct business to his firm, but his delicacy has been such that his firm have not had so much of the railroad business of Massachusetts as they would naturally have had if he had not been a railroad commissioner. I don't think it is a strong statement to make, that it has been an injury to his business that he has been a railroad commissioner. I think the facts show it. They have not done as much business for railroad companies as they had a fair right to. But you have got the figures before you, so that I have no fear, when you come to look over this matter fairly, that you will consider that Mr. Briggs has made his official position a means to secure business improperly for his own firm.

Well, then, there is another matter that has come into this case, which requires a few words of comment, and that is in respect to the Northampton bridge, and the payment of $6,000 in money by Mr. Munson. The facts disclosed in regard to it, as they appeared at first, were rather startling, and they are still a subject of highly interesting investigation for those parties more directly concerned with the matter. I do not wonder that citizens of Northampton who have paid $300,000 for a railroad, and haven't got it to-day, do and will feel a good deal of interest in pursuing that investigation. So far as Mr. Briggs is concerned, however, there are no more facts that can throw any light than those that are before you; I believe we have got to the bottom of it, as far as he is concerned. How does the matter stand? I pause not here to do more than to remind you that that contract was not with a railroad company. If there has been any such marked impropriety, as was at first suggested, we are not bound by any limit of narrow statute prohibition, but go at once to the question, whether there has been a moral wrong—a corrupt use of money. But whatever that transaction was, right or wrong, as between Mr. Munson, and Col. Lyman, and Hartwell & Co., of Northampton, I have to say, in the first place, it was no concern of Mr. Briggs, or of Mr. Smith, his partner. There is no particle of testimony here that leaves upon them a breath of suspicion of their being connected with the transaction, whether it was right or wrong. At first, when it was said that $6,000 were paid in order to induce the lowest bidder to retire from a contract in order that it might be given to a higher bidder, there seemed to be an apprehension that the higher bidder would be connected with the payment of the money; but if there is truth in man, upon the sworn testimony of Col. Lyman, Mr. Hartwell, Mr. Briggs, Mr. Smith and Mr. Munson, that transaction, whether it was right or wrong, was a transaction with which Mr. Briggs and Mr. Smith had no concern. They not only did not participate in it, but they had no knowledge of it, nor any suspicion of it. Now, upon the testimony in this case, I cannot doubt that this Committee, and every man in this community, will rest in the conviction that that transaction was one between Mr. Munson, and Col. Lyman, and Mr. Hartwell, of Northampton. That the citizens of Northampton have an honest interest to follow this matter up, I do not doubt. It is a matter of interest to them, and they are at full liberty to use all means to get at the truth, and I presume they will. But we have no concern with it.

In the next place, upon the evidence here, I must suggest to you that it is not the case that that money was paid for the motive which was first intimated to you,—the desire to get rid of a lower bidder for the contract. Simply to get rid of Messrs. Hartwell & Co., as bidders for the contract, would furnish no strong motive to Mr.

Munson's mind. There was no obligation on his part to give them the contract; on the other hand, if you will take a look at the bid they put in, and upon which they founded, I will not say their claim to the contract, but their hope of getting it, you will see that their specifications were not sufficient to found a contract upon. The bid of Messrs. Hartwell & Co. was totally silent in regard to the foundations of the bridge they wanted to build, and it was entirely insufficient as to the superstructure. There was nothing that their bid included that was sufficient to found a contract upon, except as to the masonry, and that was only sufficient by referring to the specifications of the engineer. They were not practical bridge-builders. Their bid, indeed, was a fancy bid, by a fancy firm. While, on the other hand, the testimony of Mr. Frost, the engineer, and Mr. Munson, the contractor, shows that all contractors were at liberty to furnish their own specifications; and that J. R. Smith, on making his bid, did furnish his specifications, in which he set forth in detail, not only the foundations which were to be laid and the masonry which was to be put in, but also the superstructure, the whole of which was to conform to the quality of the bridge upon the line of a first-class railroad at Seabrook and Lyme, over the Connecticut River, on the Shore Line road. And when that firm put in a bid in the way they did, if they indulged the hope of having the contract, I submit to the candor and intelligence of the Committee that no prudent contractor would ever have thought of allowing them to have it. There wasn't the foundation for making a contract. There is no evidence that Mr. Munson regarded himself under any legal obligation to pay them any money to get rid of the bid. Both Col. Lyman and Mr. Hartwell state frankly to you, that they didn't go to Mr. Munson to make any legal claim, but having an idea that they could get some money in some way. There was no legal claim, and Mr. Munson didn't recognize any legal claim.

But there was another, and a stronger, motive. Mr. Munson is a practical man. He is, so far as regards the quality of his work, a first-class contractor. He is also a man whose veracity and whose straightforwardness in his dealings are without question, and when he comes here and tells you such a story as he has told, you have a right to assume that he is telling you the truth. He has come here and given an account of the circumstances of the payment of the $6,000 to Col. Lyman and Mr. Hartwell, which commends itself to the confidence of this entire Committee. What was the situation of the case? It was this: the town of Northampton, as well as many other towns, had voted a subscription to the Massachusetts Central Railroad. I handed to Mr. Osgood a certificate from the town clerk of Northampton, showing from the official report of the action of Col. Lyman and his associates to the town of Northampton, made in March, 1875, the dates of the payments which were made by the town. In the first place, when this subscription was made, there had been numerous conditions put upon the payment of the money, but one by one, at town meetings, presided over by Luke Lyman, those conditions had been waived; and, finally, in September, 1871, and in April, 1872, the whole business of paying over the subscription was vested in a committee of three, of whom Luke Lyman was the chairman, and there was nobody else to be dealt with whenever the Massachusetts Central Railroad or Mr. Munson had occasion to go to Northampton to get their money. Luke Lyman was the man to go to. The condition of things was this: At the time of the payment to Hartwell & Co. of the $6,000, $120,000 had been paid by the town, and there had been delay after delay, town meeting after town meeting, and $180,000 remained to be paid; and other towns were failing to pay,—West Boylston, Barre, and others, and some of them have not paid to this day. It was vital to Munson and the Massachusetts Central Railroad that the town of Northampton should not fail to pay. It is nothing to say here, that the town had entered into a legal obligation to pay that money. Towns laugh at such obligations as that, and what good does a lawsuit against a town do to the Massachusetts Central Railroad! Delay was ruinous. They wanted their money, and they haven't got their money yet of some of these other towns, as the town records will show. Mr. Munson was a practical business-man. These men had helped in the matter of the loan before, and would do so again. It is not likely that they insisted upon a payment for their services; they would not do that; but they wanted money, and they came here on this fancy bid, saying they wanted that contract. They wanted $12,000, and Mr. Munson paid them $6,000 to secure their good-will. That is what Munson says, and it is no doubt strictly true. There is nothing in that transaction that shows that Mr. Smith, having made a contract to build the bridge, was any party to the payment of the $6,000. He being the lowest of a half-dozen fair bidders, who were able to do the work, why should he not do it?

So that I believe I am completely justified in saying that on the testimony before you here, Mr. Briggs stands fully clear so far as personal character is concerned. There is no imputation or censure resting upon him growing out of any participation in this transaction, and this takes us back to the question, whether or not he has been justly exposed to any censure for the construction which he has put upon the statute; and I should like to make a little discussion upon that. What construction did he put upon the statute? The words of the statute are that "no person owning stock in any railroad corporation, or in the employ of any railroad corporation, shall hold office" as commissioner or clerk. The construction that he put upon the language as applicable to him was, that it did not forbid the existing firm of A. D. Briggs & Co. from entering into contracts with railroad corporations in this State for the building of bridges for them. The question now is, whether that construction of the statute is right or wrong. This question is not a question of any actual impropriety; it is a question of the construction of the statute. There may be an actual impropriety which is not forbidden by the statute, and dealing with a railroad company may be improper, although there is no statute to forbid it; but I have already argued to you that there has been nothing in the actual transactions of Mr. Briggs which, independent of any statute, would expose him to any imputation. Now, the question is, whether there is anything in the language of the statute which forbids what he has done. If we are endeavoring to put a construction on a statute, and ascertain its true meaning, we are to submit it to a strict test, because obedience to a statute does not depend upon circumstances; it is not a matter of discretion. If this statute has such a construction as to forbid his firm building a bridge for a railroad company, then there can be no circumstances under which it ought to be done, and it is his duty to say to his firm, You must refuse applications from all railroad companies under all circumstances; you must not listen to the request of any railroad company in this State, no matter whether an accident has occurred, and a bridge has gone, and the company wants us,—no matter what the circumstances are, if the statute forbids it, we cannot entertain the proposition. And that is the construction of the law which is contended for; but it is not the construction which Mr. Briggs put upon it. Is that the true construction?

There are three classes of contracts that persons are liable to enter into with railroad corporations, which may be considered here. The first is a contract for the supply of materials alone, and that is a contract of sale. I need not argue to the Committee that when a dealer in merchandise makes a sale of merchandise to a railroad corporation, that does not bring him within the prohibition of the statute. He is a vendor, and cannot be considered in any sense in the employ of his purchaser. That, I believe, is very plain. Such dealings as that may possibly be improper. We may conceive that a railroad commissioner might possibly have transactions in the way of sale to a railroad corporation which he ought not to have; but, whether it is improper or not, it would not be within the statute prohibition, because it can never be said, with any proper use of language, that a seller of goods is in the employ of the purchaser.

There is another class of contracts, when a person agrees to furnish materials and work together. That is what was done by Mr. Briggs's firm; and I shall submit to you, gentlemen, that a contract for furnishing materials, and work, and workmen, when such personal service as may be rendered by the contractor is merely incidental to furnishing the materials, work and workmen, and is not a chief ingredient in it, is still essentially a contract of sale; it is a contract in the way of trade, and is not a contract of employment. For instance: if a railroad company wants cars, or if it wants locomotives, or if it wants rails, and wants them made to order, it is essentially a contract in the way of trade, and the personal superintendence of that contract is simply incidental to the furnishing the materials, work and workmen. Suppose a railroad company has occasion to go to a printing-office to get an advertisement inserted, or some printing done, and the proprietors of the printing-house enter into a contract to do it, would it be said that such proprietors thereby become employés of the railroad company, or rather that it is essentially a contract in the way of trade? I respectfully submit to you that all contracts of this class are simply matters of trade; exactly the same as if one of us should go to a tailor and order a suit of clothes, or direct a wagon to be made to order, or a desk for a counting-room, or any other article of the kind; although the party who agrees to do the work gives a general superintendence to it, yet, if what he does personally is not the chief element in it, but is only incidental, it is not a contract of personal service, and it does not make the contracting party in the employ of the person who is to receive the goods.

But this statute contemplates another state of things, and that is, where the personal service of the contracting party is the chief ingredient in the contract. It is this personal relation that is forbidden, and not a dealing in the way of trade. It is not easy to draw the line with absolute distinctness, so that one can always say on which side of the line a particular case will fall: we must apply our judgment to it, as in the practical affairs of life, and decide the questions as they come up. But whatever Mr. Briggs's firm has done, according to the testimony, is clearly and certainly on the right side of the line. It does not expose him in any just sense to be considered as in the employ of any railroad company.

Now, perhaps, you will think the statute ought to be broader than it is; perhaps you will think it should be amended; perhaps you will think it is wiser to make a law that will include dealings in the way of trade, as well as personal employment. So far as Mr. Briggs is concerned, I opened this case by saying, that while he claims that his conduct has not been open to just ground of objection by any citizen of this Commonwealth, no occasion even for suspicion will arise hereafter. There is no need of amendment of the statute to affect the case of Mr. Briggs, for, while believing his construction of the statute to be right, and sure he has done no wrong to any one, he will build no more bridges for our railroad companies, whether the statute is amended or not. But in determining how far the requirements of the statutes shall go, it is worthy of consideration whether, after all, the character of the man himself does not furnish the best security for the public. The chief object of special requirements of statute is to secure faithful public service. It is not wise to sacrifice the practical safety and security of the public, in a desire for a theoretical or ideal perfection. There is a passage in the speech of Milton, for unlicensed printing, which I have copied, as applicable to this question. He says: "Impunity and remissness for certain are the bane of a commonwealth; but here the great art lies, to discern in what the law is to bid restraint and punishment, and in what things persuasion only is to wish. If every action which is good or evil in man at ripe years were to be under pittance, prescription and compulsion, what were virtue but a name? . . . Banish all objects of lust, shut up all youth into the severest discipline that can be exercised in any hermitage, you cannot make them chaste that cannot thither go." So you cannot make a dishonest man into a good public officer by any statute provisions which you may make. Mr. Adams has hinted in his letter at the practical difficulties in making a law which would cover all possible cases. What you would need to provide, in order to carry out the views of some, is, that "no trustee or receiver of a railroad corporation; no person employed by such trustee or receiver; no person owning any bonds of any railroad corporation; no member of any corporation which contracts with any railroad company, or any trustee or receiver of any railroad company; no person contracting or dealing with any railroad company in the way of trade, of buying or selling, or furnishing materials or the labor of others; no person employing any railroad corporation, or any trustee or receiver of any railroad corporation, to carry freight; and no member of any corporation which so employs any railroad company, or trustee, or receiver; and generally no person directly or indirectly interested in any dealings or transactions to which any railroad company, or trustee, or receiver of any railroad company, is a party,—shall be a railroad commissioner." But this would be of no avail, if done. It would be simply—to use another illustration from Milton—"like the exploit of that gallant man who thought to pound up the crows by shutting his park gate." It is not the best way of securing faithful public service. And so it was that, two years ago, when the draft of the general railroad Act was prepared, and when this subject was adverted to in the opinions of those gentlemen who prepared it, they came to the conclusion that it was not wise to insert any further provisions in the statute.

The question remains, whether the construction of the statute by Mr. Briggs, even if wrong, should expose him to any censure. Suppose that you should be of the opinion that his construction was wrong, still, under the circumstances that he acted, doesn't he stand here fully vindicated? What were the circumstances? At the time of his appointment by Gov. Claflin, in November, 1871, there was no question raised so as to be the subject of any formal discussion in regard to the construction of the law. So Mr. Briggs testifies; Gov. Claflin does not say to the contrary. Gov. Claflin doesn't say that he had any talk with Mr. Briggs, or Mr. Briggs with him, or with anybody else upon the subject. Gov. Claflin in his letter simply expresses what is his personal impression, and given more than four years afterwards; but he doesn't undertake to state any facts or any recollection of anything in which Mr. Briggs participated in the way of a discussion. There was no question of this kind raised. But there was a question which, during the early part of the administration of Gov. Washburn, arose in the mind of Mr. Briggs, and it arose from reading the account of the examination of Mr. Appleton, in one of the legislative documents of a former year; and the question was, whether Mr. Appleton had been in the employ of a railroad corporation in this Commonwealth, according to the meaning of the statute. Now, there can be no doubt, that, at that time, there was *some* question raised in the mind of Mr. Briggs. It was a real question. It was a question which exercised his mind, and which, for a time, troubled him. It was a question upon which he talked and advised,—upon which he went to Mr. Charles Francis Adams, Jr., and the attorney-general of the Commonwealth; he had this question in his mind, and what was the question? It certainly, Mr. Chairman and gentlemen, was not, whether the fact that he had built bridges in the past twenty-five years of his occupation as a bridge-builder, was against his holding the office. That was not the question. He had built bridges all over the Commonwealth, and Gov. Claflin knew it, and Mr. Briggs's occupation was well known to the public. It was known of all men, that, in his capacity as railroad commissioner, he would have to inspect and pass upon the safety of those bridges which he had been building for twenty-five years. No man raises any question that that was so. There is no intimation that he was not to pass upon them. Gov. Claflin doesn't say it, but acknowledges it by implication. Mr. Stoddard expressly says that that was the reason of Mr. Briggs's appointment. It was to secure such a man that Gov. Claflin made the appointment. There is no evidence here on the part of anybody that the fact that he had got to inspect these bridges as a railroad commissioner was any disqualification; no question of that kind was raised at the time. What was the question, then,—was it whether or not his firm might enter into contracts with railroad corporations not chartered in Massachusetts? Was that the question which troubled his mind? Look at the statute, gentlemen. I will submit it to the candor of any gentleman of this Committee, who will take the pains to look at it,—"No person in the employ of any railroad corporation, or owning stock in any railroad corporation, shall hold either of said offices" of commissioner or clerk,—whether this had reference to railroads outside of the Commonwealth. The whole statute refers to railroads in the Commonwealth; and if you will look at the preceding sections, you will see that more than once it is expressed in plain terms, that the subject of this legislation is the railroads of the Commonwealth; and if the building of a bridge for a railroad company existing out of this State is a disqualification for Mr. Briggs holding the office of commissioner, then owning stock in a railroad corporation outside the State is also a disqualification for a commissioner. It is the same thing, Mr. Chairman. It is not possible that any lawyer or any business-man, or any man in the possession of ordinary sense, on looking at this statute, would seriously fear that this prohibition was against his engaging in the business of building bridges for companies existing outside of the Commonwealth. Nobody has ever expressed the opinion that the statute would exclude a commissioner from engaging in such work; and Mr. Pillsbury has said that nobody but a lunatic would entertain that opinion. Therefore I submit with confidence that Mr. Briggs could not entertain any fear that such work as that would bring him under the condemnation of this statute.

Well, then, what was it? He had a real question in his mind which troubled him much,—which exercised him much. It was a question founded upon the language of the statute, that "No person in the employ of a railroad corporation should hold the office of railroad commissioner"; that is to say, no person *now or hereafter* in the employ of any railroad corporation shall hold this office of commissioner. And his question was, whether he was within this prohibition. It was the only question arising under that statute, whether he could be within the prohibition of the language of the statute, if his firm should build a bridge, so that it would make him the employé of any railroad corporation in this Commonwealth. That is the question he went to Mr. Adams about; that is the question he went to the attorney-general about; and that is the question that he needed satisfaction upon.

Well, the attorney-general, in his letter to you, says that he does not consider that he gave an opinion,—a legal opinion,—because he does not call an opinion a legal opinion unless he gives it in writing. He does not consider that the statute expressly required him to give an opinion to Mr. Briggs. I am not going to quarrel with reference to this construction of language. He does not deny that he had a conversation with Mr. Briggs; and he does not deny that he said to Mr. Briggs what Mr. Briggs says he said to him; and he does not say to you now that he did then, or does now, put any different construction upon the statute from what Mr. Briggs says he put upon it. He does not say here, to-day, that his construction of that statute makes these acts of Mr. Briggs's improper. He had this conversation with Mr. Briggs, and Mr. Briggs was under the impression, and Mr. Charles Francis Adams, Jr., was under the impression, that they had got a legal opinion from the attorney-general, and the attorney-general did not inform them that he drew so fine a distinction between a legal opinion, and a conversation in which he told what his views were about the law, so that I shall submit to you that Mr. Briggs had a right to go from that conversation with the attorney-general, under the impression that he had got a legal opinion from the attorney-general as to what was proper for him to do; and he acted upon it,—he and his associates.

Well, then, on the same day, it seems that he went also and conferred with Gov. Washburn, and here, I regret to say, that there is a difference in the recollection between Gov. Washburn and Mr. Briggs; although there is no dispute upon the testimony here, as to what the conversation was between Mr. Briggs and the attorney-general, since Mr. Briggs is fortified with the statement of Mr. Charles Francis Adams, Jr.; but Gov. Washburn does not recollect the conversation he had with Mr. Briggs in the same way that Mr. Briggs recollects it; and such a failure to recollect alike, I am sorry to say, owing to the imperfection of human memory, is not a very uncommon thing in the experience of life between two perfectly honest men. We frequently see instances quite as marked as this. This conversation of only ten minutes passed out of his mind; he had entire confidence in Mr. Briggs's character; and he thought no more of it until he comes in here and gives his recollection, which is certainly entitled to consideration; and he thinks that he only expressed the opinion that Mr. Briggs's firm might properly build bridges for railroad companies outside of Massachusetts; but Mr. Briggs, on the other hand, another honest man, trustworthy, of the highest personal character, enjoying the implicit confidence of everybody that knows him, comes in and tells you what is his recollection of that conversation; and he tells you that it cannot be that he went to Gov. Washburn and put to him such a question as Gov. Washburn thinks was put to him, and the reasons which he assigns are many and strong. In the first place, he says that there was no such question in his mind; that he had no doubt upon the question which Gov. Washburn thinks he passed an opinion upon. It was not a subject of any doubt in his mind whether his firm had a right to build a bridge in Pennsylvania for a Pennsylvania railroad corporation. He thinks he could not have told Gov. Washburn what Gov. Washburn thinks he told him about his firm having not built any bridges for any railroad corporations in Massachusetts within three or four years; because the fact was not so. He also went immediately to Mr. Charles Francis Adams, Jr., who was in constant communication with Gov. Washburn, officially and otherwise, and told him what Gov. Washburn and the attorney-general had said. He thinks he put the same question to Gov. Washburn which he had put to the attorney-general, and that he got the same reply. He went away and acted upon the opinion which he got; he went away in a satisfied frame of mind; his own conviction as to the true construction of this law was confirmed. What did he do? Within less than two years, we find the lieutenant-governor of the Commonwealth and one of the executive council going to see Mr. Briggs, and inviting his firm to make proposals for the construction of three bridges on the Troy & Greenfield Railroad between the Hoosac Tunnel and North Adams; and his firm made proposals accordingly, and, in December, 1873, it appears by the letters put into this case of Mr. Frost, the chief engineer of that railroad, that these bids were laid before Gov. Washburn and the council, and remained there before them for two months. It was known by these executive officers that the firm of A. D. Briggs & Co. were making bids and proposals to build bridges, that would be under his official supervision, if they were constructed; for they were railroad bridges, and he would have to inspect them. It was a matter that was known to them, and it was never visited with any official reprobation. Mr. Briggs acted upon the conviction that his construction of the law, as derived from the attorney-general, was the true construction, and he acted upon it openly, not only in the face of the public, but with the direct knowledge of the governor and the executive council of the Commonwealth; and, further, he responded to invitations from another former member of the executive council to compete for bridges, and that is Col. Stoddard, of Worcester. Col. Stoddard was a member of the executive council in 1871, when Mr. Briggs was first appointed; and in 1872, when this question arose, in the first year of the administration of Gov. Washburn; and as soon as Col. Stoddard got out of the executive council, and had more leisure for such business, the next thing we find happening, is, that a railroad company of which he was a director, a Massachusetts company, with his knowledge, are sending for Mr. Briggs to come and make some proposals for building half a dozen bridges in Rhode Island for them. Mr. Briggs entered into contracts for doing it; and Col. Stoddard testifies here, that, having been a party to the original appointment of Mr. Briggs, and having been an executive officer during all that time, it never entered into his mind that there was any incompatibility between Mr. Briggs's position as railroad commissioner and his doing that work. Nay, more, Mr. Briggs not only in the face of day, openly, squarely, before the officers of the State, and before the public, makes these proposals, and enters into this competition, but you have the testimony of his direct competitor in business, Mr. Hawkins, that this matter was a subject of frequent discussion between Mr. Briggs and himself; and Mr. Hawkins, in those discussions, endeavored, without success, to persuade Mr. Briggs that his construction of the law was an erroneous one. In discussing this question with Mr. Hawkins, his competitor in business, Mr. Briggs took the same view as he takes now. I will here do Mr. Hawkins the justice to state, what, perhaps, I ought to have said before, that while he is the only one of Mr. Briggs's competitors in business, in Massachusetts or out of Massachusetts, who has been heard of here, before you, even he doesn't come here complaining of any actual unfairness on the part of Mr. Briggs in this respect; he confines his complaint to what he considered to be the erroneous construction of the law. Assuming that Mr. Briggs's construction of the law is right, Mr. Hawkins has nothing to complain of in his actual conduct, and he tells you so with a frankness that does him honor. Well, now, under that state of things, it appears that this construction which Mr. Briggs has adopted, is one which was adopted by him honestly and openly, after going to the best sources of information and opinion that were open to him; that it was acted upon squarely and in the face of the public, without any secrecy; and that, even if this is not, in your opinion, the true construction of the law, nevertheless it is a construction which he was justified in assuming.

Perhaps the best test of official integrity, Mr. Chairman and gentlemen, is this: that the public officer acts openly. Happy is that man who has no secrets, and who need have none. In this case, Mr. Briggs has come before you with the consciousness that, whatever has been done, has been done in the face of day, before the eyes of the officers and the people of Massachusetts; and that, so far from there having been any official disapprobation or disapproval of his conduct, he received his reappointment, in 1874, from Gov. Talbot, who had called upon him and invited him to bid for the bridges upon the Troy & Greenfield Railroad, and who had full knowledge that his firm had done so.

Now, under these circumstances, the practical questions that are to be considered before the Committee, so far as it relates to Mr. Briggs, are these: Whether the construction that he put upon the law was actually the correct construction. If you have doubts on that, then whether it was an honest construction which was adopted by him and acted upon, not secretly, but openly; and, in the next place, whether or not, in all his official conduct toward the railroad companies of this Commonwealth, his conduct has been free from any oppression or injustice, and free from any cause of censure.

I believe, now, I have gone over all that is necessary for me to say, and in closing will simply add that I entertain the belief that you will find it a duty and a pleasure and a matter of pride to leave him by your report in the full possession of his long-continued and honorable reputation, and in the confidence of the entire public, as well as in the esteem and affection of his friends, who have never wavered.

www.ingramcontent.com/pod-product-compliance
Lightning Source LLC
LaVergne TN
LVHW011146110826
845150LV00008B/2538

* 9 7 8 1 4 1 8 1 9 2 2 1 1 *